# Smart Rope JINGLES

## Jump Rope Rhymes, Raps, and Chants for Active Learning

By Rosella R. Wallace, Ph.D.

# SMARTROPE™ JINGLES
## Jump Rope Rhymes, Raps, and Chants for Active Learning

Grades 3-9
© copyright 1993 Zephyr Press, Tucson, Arizona
ISBN 0-913705-79-9

Editor: Stacey Lynn
Design and Illustration: Sheryl Shetler

# CONTENTS

# ACKNOWLEDGMENTS

Thank you to the Zap Staff and all the other SmartRopers who field-tested the jingles and raps for this book.

Thank you also to Lynn Schroeder and Sheila Ostrander, the authors of *Superlearning and Supermemory*, and Colin Rose, the author of *Accelerated Learning*. Reading their books inspired me to use brain-compatible learning and teaching methods in my classroom.

# *INTRODUCTION*

Who Can Use This Book?

PEOPLE WHO WANT TO STAY FIT AND LEARN FACTS. Many people buy this book to use as part of a personal improvement program.

CLASSROOM TEACHERS AND PARENTS. Teachers and parents have responded with great enthusiasm to this method. It makes learning more fun for your students and teaching more joyful for you. You do not need to feel guilty or that you are fudging on "time on task." Active learning is playing while learning and learning while playing. It is "purposeful play." It fosters integrated education and cooperative learning.

SPECIAL EDUCATION TEACHERS, STUDENTS, AND PARENTS OF SPECIAL EDUCATION STUDENTS. This kinesthetic approach often works for people with special learning needs. Special education teachers involved in the Collaborative Model have introduced the method into classrooms to promote success for all students. They are reporting encouraging research results with fetal alcohol- and drug-affected children as well as other children with brain damage.

GIFTED PROGRAMS. Teachers of gifted students have used this method to help students learn facts quickly and easily. It gives all students more time for problem solving and creativity.

CROSS-CULTURAL EDUCATION. SmartRaps work well with drumming. This variation is used in some schools in Alaska. Fun, laughter, and the fellowship of large groups bridge the gap between cultures until it melts away.

PHYSICAL EDUCATION TEACHERS. Include SmartRope jingles with your jump rope program and SmartRaps with your aerobic dance class.

HOME SCHOOLERS. Home schoolers have been staunch supporters of Active Learning. Most households have jump ropes and welcome the variety and chance to be both active and creative.

E.S.L. (English as a second language) or L.E.P. (limited English proficient) STUDENTS. SmartRaps and SmartRope jingles are rhythmic expressions of standard English. In addition to teaching facts related to the lesson, the natural rhythm and intonation patterns of conversational American English used in these activities make them some of the more innovative and exciting approaches to language learning that have been produced to date.

GIRL SCOUTS AND BOY SCOUTS. Both Girl Scouts and Boy Scouts are using SmartRope jingles in their rope-skipping tournaments and leagues. Many councils provide the opportunity to earn incentive patches for participating in rope-skipping programs and events. These organizations recognize the importance of this sport that encourages participation and is flexible in providing for the needs of each child. Competitive rope skipping is a relatively new sport, but it has been rapidly gaining popularity.

## THE POWER OF WORDS

I discovered the power of jump rope chants with learning lyrics while teaching in elementary school. The lessons for the week included using numbers to write dates. Before I could teach my students to do that, I needed to make certain that they all knew the months of the year in the correct order. I discovered a few did not. I tried the usual methods of repetition in class and sending a list home, hoping the parents would help. Even though the students were trying, they still weren't having any luck memorizing the months.

These students liked to jump rope during recess. They often chanted "Cinderella, dressed in yella . . ." and some of the other old standards. That gave me the idea to chant the months while jumping rope. It worked like magic! The kids liked having their teacher get involved in rope jumping and they liked the new month chant as well as the oldies. In a very short time, they could all recite the months and we could go on with the date lesson.

When I saw how well it worked for the months, I started using the technique for teaching other facts that students need to know, such as the multiplication tables.

Chanting words to the rhythm of jumping rope has been a favorite pastime of children around the world. Why not make the chants have learning lyrics? It's just as much fun (some say more) and accomplishes three goals at once: FACTS, FUN, AND FITNESS.

SmartRaps are a variation without using jump ropes. They can be used indoors and in all classrooms. Rappin' is a rhythmic repetitive chant accompanied by finger snapping or hand clapping. The rhythm makes your whole body want to get into the act and, because of the learning lyrics, engages the whole brain as well.

Chanting the learning lyrics while jumping or moving around engages the auditory and kinesthetic systems. The rhythms and rhymes of the chants together with the rhythmic movement accelerate learning because they facilitate memory.

## ACTIVE LEARNING

It is not intended that this material be used exclusively to cover subject areas. The activities that I have included for specific subjects are to be used with your regular lesson plans for variety, to encourage participation, and to relieve stress, all of which accelerate learning.

Some of the material is a result of teachers' requests. The states and their capitals are an example. I deliberately broke the material into small chunks instead of putting it all in one long rap or jingle. George Miller pointed out in a paper entitled "The Magical Number Seven: Plus or Minus Two" that the immediate memory is limited in the number of items it can hold. It is best to break large amounts of material into manageable chunks. If the chunks can be rhythmical, that's even better.

Is the learning of facts really that important in this day and age when problem solving has become the focus? Memorizing can help students absorb and retain factual information on which understanding and critical thought depend. Without rapid and accurate recall of bodies of specific knowledge, the more sophisticated mental operations of analysis, synthesis, and evaluation are impossible.

## *HOW TO USE THIS BOOK*

Have fun with SmartRope jingles and SmartRaps. Each can be either a jump-rope activity or a rap (rhythmical recitation). Change the way you use the learning lyrics to suit your situation. If a SmartRope jingle calls for you to squat down or turn around, you can do the same movements for a SmartRap. Here are a few ways that learners love to use Active Learning.

REVIEW JOYFULLY. Turn small blocks of time into a joyful review time. Example: If you have a few minutes before the lunch bell rings, recite a SmartRap while waiting. Students will participate because it is fun. It will not be looked upon as a dreaded review.

COMBINE PLAY TIME WITH LEARNING TIME. Turn play time on the playground and at home into a combination of play time/learning time, with SmartRope jingles and Smart-Raps.

PERFORMANCES FOR ASSEMBLIES OR PROGRAMS. Use the jingles and raps for performances. Kids love to ham it up and show off their jump-rope skills or rhythmical movements while reciting the learning lyrics. Parents appreciate the combination of performing and learning. This material is ideal for assemblies and school programs. Special talents, such as dancing or singing, are not required.

SMALL-GROUP ACTIVITIES. Let each group work together on a SmartRap to demonstrate or teach to the class. I have seen children get so involved in this type of project that they meet during recesses and after school to perfect their demonstrations.

CHEERS. Everyone loves to be a cheerleader. Show your students how to make pom-pons by covering toilet paper tubes with crepe paper. Glue or staple strips of crepe paper on each end. Now students can work together using the learning lyrics as cheers. The groups can take turns being the cheerleaders, and the rest of the class their cheering section. All set? You bet! Ready-o, let's go!

CREATIVE WRITING. Encourage children to make up their own learning lyrics or add to or modify the ones in this book. This activity makes a good creative writing lesson. It promotes the integration of subjects and teaching across the curriculum.

PHYSICAL EDUCATION. Active learning can be used as a part of the physical education program. Some schools use the SmartRope jingles in conjunction with their P.E. jump-rope program. Others use the SmartRaps as part of their aerobic dance classes.

GIRL SCOUTS' AND BOY SCOUTS' ROPE-SKIPPING PROGRAMS. The Girl Scouts and Boy Scouts use SmartRope jingles in their rope-skipping leagues and tournaments. Some combine the jingles with the different rope-skipping "tricks" they need to accomplish in order to earn special badges.

FREE-TIME REWARD. Kids love the opportunity to interact with their peers. If my students win "free time" as a reward, I usually give them several activities to choose from. Often they choose either to write new raps and jingles or to practice the ones we used recently.

MUSIC. Set new or existing learning lyrics to the tunes of familiar songs or make up original music for the learning lyrics. Music makes the jingles even easier to remember.

## HOW CAN I BE CERTAIN I HAVE THE CORRECT BEAT?

The SmartRope jingles and SmartRaps are not always written in a "poetically correct" style. There is more than one way to recite the chants, depending on various factors such as the tempo of your personal rope skipping, the motions you choose to add to a rap, the length of the material (if the jump rope jingle is long, you will want to jump at a slower pace so you won't get too tired), and your own personal style of chanting.

For this reason, there is not a "correct rhythm." The rhythm is flexible and the words can be manipulated to fit your needs. At times, you may even want to add some words or leave some out to fit your style. The chants and raps have been field-tested. I found that people used them in a variety of ways, but this did not decrease their effectiveness. The object is to have fun while learning in a stress-free manner.

Start by saying the words to the beat you choose while snapping your fingers or tapping your toes. Let your body feel the rhythm, and the words will slide in at the right places.

# SmartRopers

SmartRopers, SmartRopers—
We're really cool.
We know the facts.
We're nobody's fool.

We like to chant
And jump rope too—
Rappin' and jumpin'
The whole day through.

Our raps are facts
We need to know.
The SmartRope helps;
It's the way to go.

SmartRopers stay fit.
SmartRopers have fun.
SmartRopers are smart.
What have we done?

Facts, fun, and fitness—
We've combined the three.
SmartRope jingles are
The magic key!

# *Our Place*

Country, continent;
Planet, galaxy.
Our country is the United States;
Our continent North America.
We live on the planet Mother Earth
In the galaxy Milky Way.
Country, continent,
Planet, galaxy.

# *The Planets\**

My Verse Easily Makes Jumping Students
Utter Nine Planets.
Mercury, Venus, Earth, Mars, Jupiter,
Saturn, Uranus, Neptune, Pluto

> \*The first letter of each word gives a clue for the planets
> in the order of their distance from the sun.

# The Moon

The moon is the Earth's
Only natural satellite.
One-fourth the size of Earth,
It brightens up our night.

It revolves around the Earth in
Twenty-nine and one-half days.
Moon shines because it reflects
The light from our sun's rays.

Neil Armstrong was the first man
On the moon to walk.
His words were oh-so-sweet
When he made that famous talk.

As all the world did listen,
The year was nineteen sixty-nine.
"That's one small step for man,
One giant leap for mankind."

# *Directions Rap*

A compass rose is a symbol.
You find it on a map.

Letters N, E, S, W
Are in our Directions Rap.

N. E. S. W.
North, east, south, west.

North, east, south, west,
Chant directions with some zest.

Nobody Ever Sees Woozles—
North, east, south, west.

We've looked in all directions—
North, east, south, west.

North, east, south, west.
I can pass the directions test.

# The Oceans

Large bodies of salt water
Cover much of the Earth.

They are known as the oceans.
To name them has much worth.

Can you name all the oceans?
There are only four.

The Pacific, the Atlantic,
The Indian, and the Arctic.

We've named all the oceans;
There aren't any more.

The Marina Trench is the deepest
Place on the ocean floor.

It's in the great Pacific,
The largest of the four.

The Pacific, the Atlantic,
The Indian, and the Arctic.

We've named all the oceans;
There aren't any more.

# Continents Rap

Seven big pieces
Of land to share.

Called continents,
They need our care.
    North America,
    South America,
    Europe, and
    Asia, too.
    Africa,
    Australia,
    Antarctica, too.
I can name all seven for you.

I like to name the continents,
Point to them on the map.

Snap your fingers; tap your toes.
Here's our Continents Rap.
    North America,
    South America,
    Europe, and
    Asia, too.
    Africa,
    Australia,
    Antarctica, too.
I can name all seven for you.

# "A" States and Capitals

A, Alabama,
Capital, Montgomery.
A, Alaska,
Capital, Juneau.
Jumpers, name the
States you know.

A, Alabama,
Capital, Montgomery.
A, Alaska,
Capital, Juneau.
We're A-OK.
We're on the go!

A, Arizona,
Capital, Phoenix.
A, Arkansas,
Capital, Little Rock.
Yes, yes,
Let's take stock.

Alabama, Montgomery.
Alaska, Juneau.
Arizona, Phoenix.
Arkansas, Little Rock.
States and capitals,
"A" states talk.

# "C" and "D" States and Capitals

California,
Colorado,
Connecticut,
Delaware,
What are the capitals of
These states so fair?

California, Sacramento.
Colorado, Denver.
Connecticut, Hartford.
Delaware, Dover.
You've got it!
Say them over.

California, Sacramento.
Colorado, Denver.
Connecticut, Hartford.
Delaware, Dover.
The "C" and "D" states,
Move it on over.

# "F," "G," and "H" States and Capitals

F, G, H.
F, Florida.
G, Georgia.
H is for Hawaii.
F, G, H.
There are just three.

F, Florida,
Tallahassee.
G, Georgia,
Atlanta.
H, Hawaii,
Honolulu.

Hawaii is
The fiftieth state
Hawaii,
Honolulu.
Hawaii, Hawaii—
In rank, it's new.

# "I" States and Capitals

Idaho, Illinois,
Indiana, Iowa.
Idaho, Illinois,
Indiana, Iowa.
Four "I" states,
Last is Iowa.

Idaho, Boise.
Illinois, Springfield.
Next Indiana,
And Indianapolis,
Iowa, Des Moines.
Knowing is pure bliss.

# "K" and "L" States and Capitals

K, Kansas.
K, Kentucky.
L, Louisiana.
Two Ks, one L—
K, K, L.
We know them well.

Kansas, Topeka.
Kentucky, Frankfort.
Louisiana,
Baton Rouge.
Did you say Scrooge?
No, Baton Rouge!

# The First Four "M" States and Capitals

Maine, Maryland,
Massachusetts, Michigan.
Maine, Maryland,
Massachusetts, Michigan.
The first four M states—
Learning them is fun.

Maine, Augusta.
Maryland, Annapolis.
Massachusetts, Boston.
Michigan, Lansing.
The capitals, we know them.
We're proud; we're prancing.

# The Last Four "M" States and Capitals

Minnesota,
Mississippi,
Missouri,
Montana.
We all know them,
Including Hanna.

Minnesota, St. Paul.
Mississippi, Jackson.
Missouri's capital
Is Jefferson City.
Montana's is Helena.
Now aren't we witty!

# The First Four "N" States and Capitals

Nebraska,
Nevada,
New Hampshire,
New Jersey.
Four "N" states
We'd like to see.

Nebraska, Lincoln.
Nevada, Carson City.
New Hampshire, Concord.
New Jersey, Trenton.
Learning capitals,
Hey, this is fun!

# The Last Four "N" States and Capitals

New Mexico,
New York,
North Carolina,
North Dakota.
Two "Norths," two "News."
I want a soda.

New Mexico, Santa Fe.
New York, Albany.
North Carolina, Raleigh.
North Dakota, Bismarck.
North, North, New, New,
Learning is a lark!

# "O" States and Capitals

Three O's:
Ohio,
Oklahoma,
Oregon.
Oh, oh, oh,
Just for fun.

Ohio, Columbus.
Oklahoma,
Oklahoma City.
Oregon, Salem.
Beautiful O's,
Let's see some.

# "P," "R," and "S" States and Capitals

P, Pennsylvania.
R, Rhode Island.
S, South Carolina.
S, South Dakota.
Only two "Souths,"
That's the quota.

Pennsylvania,
Harrisburg.
Rhode Island,
Providence.
South Carolina,
Columbia.

South Dakota,
Pierre.
P, R, S
States,
We've learned
Our share!

# "T," "U," and "V" States and Capitals

Tennessee,
Texas,
Utah, Vermont,
Virginia last.
T, U, V states,
Say them fast.

Tennessee, Nashville.
Texas, Austin.
Utah, Salt Lake City.
Vermont, Montpelier.
Virginia, Richmond.
The facts are clear.

# "W" States and Capitals

Washington,
West Virginia,
Wisconsin,
Then Wyoming.
Four "W" states,
Chant and swing.

Washington, Olympia.
West Virginia, Charleston.
Wisconsin, Madison.
Wyoming, Cheyenne.
Four "W" states,
Say 'em—we can!

# Our United States

The smallest state
Is Rhode Island.
The largest state
Is Alaska, so grand.

The largest city
In the United States
Is New York City.
It "number 1" rates.

State with the
Largest population
Is California
In our nation.

# *Deserts of the World*

This desert chant is SAGA K.
A third of the Earth is desert today.
Chant     SAGA K     SAGA K
Some are hot deserts; some are cold.
The five main deserts, we are told,
Are     SAGA K     SAGA K

Sahara,     Arabian,

Gobi,     Australian.

Take a safari to the Kalahari.

K for Kalahari.

SAGA K     SAGA K

Sahara, Arabian, Gobi, Australian, and

Kalahari. That's the way!

# *Islands of the World*

An island is surrounded by $H_2O$.
Smaller than a continent, we all know:
Good News Goes By Mail,  G  N  G  B  M.
To four large islands near and far,
From Greenland to Madagascar,
Good News Goes By Mail,  G  N  G  B  M.
Greenland, New Guinea,
Borneo, and Madagascar,
Surrounded by water, yes they are.

# *Addition and Subtraction*

Addition tells the total
When two or more groups
Are put together.
The answer is always bigger
In any kind of weather.

Subtraction tells what's left
When things in a group
Are taken away.
The answer is always smaller,
At any time of the day.

# Even and Odd Numbers

Do you know if a number
Is even or odd?

Even or odd?
Even or odd?

It is easy to tell
With this math mod.

Look at the last part—
There's the clue.

Makes it easy
For me and you.

If numbers end in
0, 2, 4, 6, or 8,

They're even numbers.
Isn't that great?

If numbers don't end in
0, 2, 4, 6, or 8,

Then they're odd numbers.
That's their fate.

# *Count by Twos*

Zero, two, four
Six, and eight.

Counting by twos
Is really great.

Ten, twelve, fourteen,
Sixteen, eighteen,

Twenty is next;
We're celebrating.

2, 4, 6, 8, 10, 12, 14, 16, 18, 20

# *Count by Threes*

Count by threes.
Touch your knees.

Three, six, nine.
You're doin' fine.

Twelve, fifteen, eighteen.
We're still waiting.

Twenty-one, twenty-four.
Chant some more.

Twenty-seven, thirty.
We're not nerdy.

Count by threes.
It's a breeze.

3, 6, 9, 12, 15, 18, 21, 24, 27, 30

Counting by threes
Is a breeze.

# *Count by Fours*

Count by fours.
Point at doors.

Four, eight, twelve,
Sixteen, twenty,

Twenty-four, twenty-eight,
Thirty-two, thirty-six.

Count by fours.
We know the tricks.

4, 8, 12, 16, 20, 24, 28, 32, 36

Count by fours.
We know the tricks!

# Count by Fives

Count by fives.
It really jives.

Each one ends
In five or zero.

Count by fives.
You'll be a hero.

5, 10, 15, 20, 25, 30, 35, 40, 45, 50

Count by fives.
Wow, that's nifty!

# *Count by Sixes*

Each time you count,
You just add six.

Six, six, just add six.
Mix, mix, a cake you mix.

6, 12, 18, 24, 30, 36, 42, 48, 54, 60

Six times nine
Is fifty-four.

Six times ten,
Just add six more.

6, 12, 18, 24, 30, 36, 42, 48, 54, 60

Multiply, multiply.
Reach for the sky!

# Count by Sevens

Count by sevens.
You'll find it fun.

Add seven each time
Until you're done.

7, 14, 21, 28, 35, 42, 49, 56, 63, 70

Seven times two is fourteen.
Seven times three is twenty-one.

Seven times four is twenty-eight.
Keep on going; this is fun.

Seven times five is thirty-five.
Seven times six is forty-two.

Seven times seven is forty-nine.
Multiplying sevens, doin' fine.

Seven times eight is fifty-six.
Seven times nine is sixty-three.

Seven times ten is seventy.
Sevens are easy for you and me.

# *Count by Eights*

Each time add eight.
Stand up straight.

Eight, sixteen,
Twenty-four, thirty-two.

You like me and
I like you.

Forty, forty-eight,
Fifty-six, sixty-four.

Count by eights.
There are still two more.

Nine times eight
Is seventy-two.

Next is eighty.
Now we're through!

8, 16, 24, 32, 40, 48, 56, 64, 72, 80

# Count by Nines

Each time you count
Just add a nine.

Counting by nines
Will work out fine.

Nine, eighteen,
Twenty-seven, thirty-six.

Nines are fun when
You know the tricks.

Forty-five, fifty-four,
Sixty-three, seventy-two.

Nine times nine is
Eighty-one.

Ninety is the last.
Job well done!

9, 18, 27, 36, 45, 54, 63, 72, 81, 90

# *Geometry*

A triangle has three sides, three sides.

A rectangle has four sides, four sides.

A pentagon has five sides, five sides.

A hexagon has six sides, six sides.

An octagon has eight sides, eight sides.

Triangle three, triangle three.
Triangle three. Easy for me.

Rectangle four, rectangle four.
Rectangle four. Learn some more.

Pentagon five, pentagon five.
Pentagon five. Jump and jive.

Hexagon six, hexagon six.
Hexagon six. Know the tricks.

Octagon eight, octagon eight.
Octagon eight. Be my date!

# Roman Numerals

Clocks, dates,
Outlines. Hey!
Roman numerals
Are used today.

I for one,
V for five,
X for ten.
Swing and jive.

L for fifty,
C, one hundred,
D, five hundred.
Have you wondered?

M, one thousand.
Thousand, you say?
Roman numerals,
Still used today.

# Measuring

Twelve inches in a foot.
Three feet in a yard.

Say it again.
It's not hard.

Twelve inches in a foot.
Three feet in a yard.

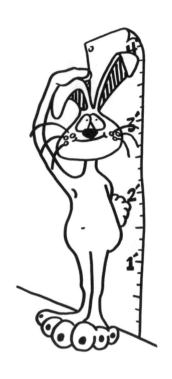

Measuring length,
You've got it, Pard.

Five thousand two hundred
Eighty feet are in a mile.

Five thousand two hundred
Eighty feet makes you smile.

Five thousand two hundred
Eighty feet are in a mile.

Measuring length
In a rappin' style.

# *Liquid Measure*

It takes two cups to fill a pint.
Two cups and one pint are the same.
You can call two cups one pint—
It's the same with a different name.

It takes two pints to fill a quart.
Two pints and one quart are the same.
You can call two pints one quart.
It's OK in the measuring game.

It takes four quarts to fill a gallon.
Four quarts and one gallon are the same.
You can call four quarts a gallon.
You'll be known for measuring fame.

# Dry Measure

Sixteen ounces in a pound.
Sixteen ounces in a pound.
Dry measure, dry measure
Facts I've found.

Two thousand pounds
Are in a ton.
Two thousand pounds
Are in a ton.

How many ounces in a pound?
Sixteen, sixteen. This is fun.
How many pounds in a ton?
Two thousand pounds in a ton!

Sixteen ounces in a pound.
Two thousand pounds in a ton.
We learn facts while
We jump and run.

# Perimeter

Perimeter, perimeter
Is the distance around
A geometric figure
Or a plot of ground.

To find the perimeter
Add the length of all the sides.
Add up the length of all the sides.
Remember those perimeter guides.

# Area

Number of square units
That cover a figure is
The area, the area.
I'm a measuring whiz.

Area of a rectangle:
You must multiply
Length times width.
Easy, breathe a sigh.

Area of a triangle,
Multiply one-half
Base times height.
Easy, makes me laugh.

# Time

How many seconds in a minute?
Sixty, sixty is the limit.

How many minutes in an hour?
Sixty, sixty, sweet and sour.

How many hours in a day?
Twenty-four—sleep, work, and play.

How many days in a week?
Seven for kind words to speak.

How many days in a year?
Three hundred sixty-five for good cheer.

How many weeks in a year?
Fifty-two, free from fear.

How many months in a year?
Twelve, the calendar makes clear.

How many years in a decade?
Ten years for you to have it made.

A century is one hundred years.
By that time, old age nears.

A millennium is one thousand years.
A long, long time to you, my dears.

# Minutes

Sixty minutes are in an hour.
Chant and rhyme for memory power.

Thirty minutes in a half hour.
Rhyme and chant for memory power.

Fifteen minutes, a quarter hour.
Repeat, repeat for memory power.

Sixty minutes in an hour.
Thirty minutes in a half hour.

Fifteen minutes, a quarter hour.
We know time. Yo, memory power!

# Days of the Week

A week is seven days.
A week is seven days.
Take care of every day.
Enjoy your work. Enjoy your play.

Start each day with a smile
And try to help someone.
It will be a good day
For working and for fun.

Sunday, Monday,
Tuesday, Wednesday,
Thursday, Friday,
And Saturday.

# *Months of the Year*

A month, about thirty days.
Each month is a new chance.
A month, about thirty days
To jump and sing and dance.

January, February, March,
April, May, and June,
July, August, September,
October, November, December.

Twelve months are in a year.
Twelve months are in a year.
Be thankful for each month.
Fill them with joy and cheer.

# *Writing Time*

"Ante" is Latin for "before."
Think A, B: Ante, Before.
Ante, Before.
Touch the floor.

"After" in Latin is "post."
Think P comes after A.
After is post.
Give a toast.

"Meridian" is Latin for "noon."
Think M, N: Meridian, Noon.
Meridian, Noon.
Turn around soon.

Ante, Before. Meridian, Noon.
A.M.: Before noon.
A.M. Before.
Touch the floor.

Post, After. Meridian, Noon.
P.M.: After noon.
After is post.
Give a toast.

A.M. is before noon.
P.M. is after noon.
Know some Latin—
A timely boon.    **50**

# Apostrophes

Use an apostrophe in a contraction
To show that letters are left out.
Makes two words into one word,
That's what contractions are all about.

Use an apostrophe to show possession.
Tim's book belongs to Tim.
The apostrophe shows ownership.
The book does not belong to Jim.

Use "s" apostrophe with plural nouns—
Shows more than one has ownership.
"S" apostrophe in rappers' SmartRaps.
MANY rappers; that's the tip.

# Periods

Periods come after an initial
And an abbreviation,
Like U.S.A. for our great nation.

Use a period to end a sentence
That a fact does state
Or gives a command, like "Don't be late."

# *Colons*

One above the other
Are the two dots of the colon.
To introduce a list of items,
The colon gets you rollin'.

After the salutation
In a business letter;
A colon is the one to use—
Makes a business letter better.

In a bibliography,
Between the publication place
And the publisher, we put
A colon in that space.

Three good uses for a colon:
To introduce a list,
Bibliography, business letter.
Now you've got the gist!

# *Hyphens*

A hyphen is a
Short, straight line
For writing numbers
Twenty-one to ninety-nine.

If you must divide a word
At the end of a line,
You can use a hyphen.
It will be just fine.

# *End Punctuation*

Four kinds of sentences;
Three end in "-tive":
Declarative, imperative, and interrogative.

Four kinds of sentences;
One ends in "-tory,"
Shows strong feeling: exclamatory.

A declarative sentence states a fact.
It ends with a period.
I will use tact.

An imperative sentence gives a command.
It ends with a period.
Now everyone stand.

Interrogative sentence a question asks.
Ends with a question mark.
Have you done the tasks?

Exclamatory, surprise or feeling strong,
Needs an exclamation point.
Look out!  That's wrong!

Declarative, imperative, interrogative,
Explanatory. That's the story.
Know which ending to give.

# The Largest and Loudest Animal

Largest animal, great blue whale,
It makes the loudest sound.
Loudest animal, great blue whale,
Largest and loudest around!

Largest animal of all time—
One hundred ten feet long.
Has a thick layer of blubber,
Is a swimmer, swift and strong.

Great blue's voice can be heard
For five hundred thirty miles,
Almost two hundred decibels strong!
Has distinctive singing styles.

Great blue whale, largest animal,
Make yourself real long!
Great blue whale, loudest animal,
Yell with a voice so strong!

# The Tallest and Largest Land Animals

Big land animals—
Tallest, giraffe,
Largest, elephant.
Hear me call.

The tallest animal
With a long neck
Is a giraffe—
Twenty feet tall.

Largest land animal—
African elephant.
Over six tons,
He's no doll.

Tallest, giraffe,
Largest, elephant.
SmartRope jumpers,
Have a ball!

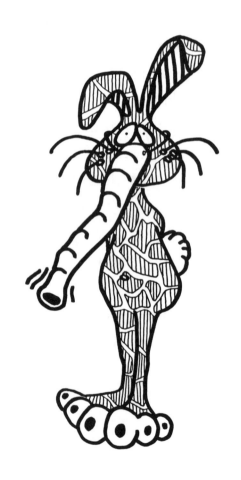

# Fantastic Birds

Which fantastic birds
Fly the farthest,
Fastest, highest?
Can you say?

Farthest flying bird:
The Arctic tern.
Eleven thousand
Miles each way.

Fastest flying bird:
Peregrine falcon.
Two hundred miles per hour
Any old day.

Highest flying bird:
Bar-headed goose.
Twenty-five thousand
Feet they say.

Travels far—tern.
Fastest—falcon.
Highest—goose.
Birds—hurray!

# The Largest Insects

Two largest insects:
Goliath beetle,
Hercules moth.
Tell me more.

Two largest insects:
Goliath beetle,
Inches long?
More than four!

Hercules moth,
Wingspan of
Eleven inches.
It can soar!

Two largest insects:
Goliath beetle,
Hercules moth.
Insect lore.

# The Largest Bird and Fish

The largest bird is
African ostrich—
Nine feet tall.
Tall, I'd say.

The largest fish is
A whale shark.
Fifteen tons
He does weigh.

The largest bird is
African ostrich.
The largest fish is
A whale shark.

Large bird—ostrich.
Large fish—whale shark.
SmartRope jumpers,
This is a lark!

# The Largest Snake and Reptile

The largest snake is
The anaconda—
Five hundred pounds.
Wow! Large snake.

The largest reptile,
A crocodile,
Lives in salt water,
Not in a lake.

The largest snake is
The anaconda;
The largest reptile,
The crocodile.

Snake—anaconda.
Reptile—crocodile.
SmartRope jumpers
Jump with style!

# Smallest Plant, Largest Plant

The smallest plant
Is a diatom—
One ten-thousandth
Of an inch.

SmartRope jumpers,
Get small, squat down.
Be a diatom, diatom,
It's a cinch!

The largest plant is
A sequoia tree.
General Sherman
Is its name.

SmartRope jumpers,
Stretch up tall
Like the sequoia
Tree of fame.

# Vertebrates

A vertebrate is an animal
That has a backbone.

A man is one.
He's not alone.

Mammals and birds
Are vertebrates, too.

They're warm-blooded,
Like me and you.

Warm-blooded vertebrates,
Are birds and mammals.

Mammals have hair,
Like dogs and camels.

Cold-blooded vertebrates
Have different styles.

Amphibians and fish
And also reptiles.

Mammals, birds, reptiles,
Amphibians, and fish.

You know all the vertebrates.
You've got your wish!

# *Rainbow Colors*

Remember the name
ROY G. BIV.
The letters in this name
A clue will give.

Red, Orange, Yellow,
Green, and Blue,
Indigo and Violet—
The rainbow hue.

# Clouds

Cirrus clouds high
In the atmosphere form.
Made of ice crystals,
Wispy is their norm.

Like layers or sheets
Are the clouds called stratus.
Nearer to the Earth,
Drizzle is their status.

Cumulus clouds are
Often flat on the bottom,
Piled up heaps of white
Cauliflower-shaped cotton.

Nimbus clouds are
Uniformly dark gray.
They bring us snowstorms
Or a wet, rainy day.

# Water Cycle

Water travels from
Place to place.
SmartRope jumpers,
Keep the pace.

### E VAP O RA TION

Water vapor gets
Into the air
From oceans, lakes, rivers,
From water everywhere.

### TRAN SPI RA TION

Plants release water—
They transpire.
Water in the air;
They never tire.

### PRE CIP I TA TION

Rain, snow, sleet, hail
Soaks in the ground,
Runs to the oceans.
It goes round and round.

Evaporation
Transpiration
Precipitation
The Water Cycle!

# Climates

Climate is the average weather
Over a long period of time.
There are some basic types of climates.
Let's rap this climate rhyme.

Temperate zone has four seasons.
The arctic is nearly always cold.
A desert clime is usually dry,
But climates vary, I've been told.

# Tropics

Near the equator are the tropics—
Tropical wet or tropical wet and dry.
They get the direct rays of the sun.
They are warmest. You can see why.

Tropical wet has heavy rain
All throughout the year—
Rainy, rainy all year long.
People need rain gear.

Tropical wet and dry has
Monsoon rains for part of the time.
The rest of the year is dry.
Hot and dry, tropical clime.

# Layers of the Earth

There are three layers of Earth.
    Hop, hop.

The CRUST, the MANTLE, the CORE.
    Hop, hop.
The CRUST, the MANTLE, the CORE.

At the center of the Earth,
Molten rock does form a CORE
Two thousand two hundred
Miles thick. Let's jump some more.

The MANTLE surrounds the core.
Mostly solid, but still hot.
One thousand eight hundred
Miles thick. Golly, that's a lot!

Slowly as the Earth cooled,
A thin crust formed over the top.
The earth is still cooling.
The CRUST gives us a place to hop.

The CRUST, the MANTLE, the CORE.
    Hop, hop.
The CRUST, the MANTLE, the CORE.

# The Solar System

Comets, asteroids, and meteors—
At the center is the sun.
Nine planets and their moons—
Revolving every one.

Our sun is one of billions of stars
In the galaxy Milky Way.
It's a glowing ball of hot gases.
It warms the Earth every day.

Nine planets revolve around the sun.
Some are rocky like Earth and Mars.
Others like Jupiter and Saturn
Are balls of gas more like the stars.

Don't forget a belt of asteroids,
Small planets, near Earth and Mars.
When they collide and break into pieces,
They're meteors or "falling stars."

The large ones sometimes don't burn up.
These are called meteorites.
They form craters when they hit Earth,
They're found at several sites.

# Comets

Comets are made of
Dust and gases.

Like dirty snowballs,
These frozen masses

Travel their orbits
Around the sun.

Halley's Comet is
The most famous one.

Everyone watches
When it appears,

Once about every
Seventy-six years.

# Rocks

Three main types of rocks
In different ways were formed.
Rocks are made of minerals.
By heat they all were warmed.

Igneous, sedimentary,
Metamorphic are
The three main classes.
We'll remember them, by gar!

Some examples of igneous
Are obsidian and granite, too.
Formed from cooling magma,
Molten rock that looks like goo.

Sandstone, limestone, conglomerate
Are sedimentary rocks.
Changed by heat and pressure,
Contain fossils, shale, and chalks.

Mountain-building pressure,
And changed by melting heat.
Marble, slate, and schist
Are metamorphic rocks so neat.

# Human Body Systems

Our body is a miracle,
With body systems major.
Each has different parts
And does its job, I'll wager.

Memorize this sentence.
It will help your memory.
First letters are the clues,
The nine body systems' key.

Each Day Research Reveals New Methods,
Saving Us Chores.

Each - E - Endocrine
Day - D - Digestive
Research - R - Respiratory
Reveals - R - Reproductive
New - N - Nervous
Methods - M - Muscular
Saving - S - Skeletal
Us - U - Urinary
Chores - C - Circulatory

Body systems!  Body systems!
We just recited nine.
When they all work in unity,
Our body feels so fine!

# The Muscular System

Two different kinds of muscles
Are in the body's muscular system.
Some are and some aren't controlled by
    thoughts.
Listen, we can list 'em!

The <u>voluntary</u> muscles first.
They are controlled by thought.
Move the bones of the skeleton—
We use them every day a lot.

Muscles not controlled by thought
Are called <u>involuntary.</u>
Some move food to be digested;
Heart pumps blood for them to carry.

Keep both kinds of muscles healthy;
Eat good food and exercise.
Voluntary and involuntary,
Strong muscles are a prize.

# The Circulatory System

Circulatory system consists of
Blood vessels, blood, and heart.
Supplies oxygen and nutrients
And carries away the waste part.

The pulse is the number of times
Your heart in each minute does beat—
About seventy times each minute
For an adult resting in a seat.

Heart pumps about five quarts of blood
During that same minute.
It circulates throughout our bod
Oxygen and nutrients in it.

Blood vessels include arteries,
Carry blood from the heart to each cell.
Eat a balanced diet with iron
To keep those blood cells well.

Veins carry blood from cells to heart;
Capillaries connect arteries to veins.
About sixty thousand miles of vessels
Work together, without strains.

# The Respiratory System

Lungs and other organs of breathing
Make up the system respiratory.
Oxygen from air to blood—
The respiratory story.

Carbon dioxide from the blood is waste.
It is what the lungs do take;
They release it back into the air.
Plants use it—for goodness' sake.

A resting adult breathes
About twelve times each minute.
Daily two thousand six hundred gallons
   of air—
We need the oxygen in it.

Our lungs prefer only fresh, clean air.
They say to us, "Please don't smoke!"
It's a dumb thing to do because
Lung cancer is not a joke!

# *The Digestive System*

The digestive system takes in food
And turns it into nutrients,
Which are carried by the blood to cells.
It makes a lot of sense.

Food mixes with saliva
In the mouth while being chewed.
This prepares food for the body's use,
Whether raw, fried, fresh, or stewed.

Food passes through the esophagus.
To the stomach it will go,
Where it is stored and broken down
For nourishment, we know.

Twenty-two feet of small intestine,
Then finishes the digestion.
Nutrients pass into the bloodstream
Without instruction or suggestion.

The large intestine eliminates
Food the body cannot digest.
This great digestive system
Keeps us going—gives us zest!

# *The Nervous System*

Nervous system consists of
Sense organs, nerves, and brain.
Brain regulates our body,
The controller, Mr. Main.

Five senses are sight, hearing,
Smell, touch, and taste.
They send messages to the brain
Instantly—no time to waste.

From these senses and the nerves
The brain takes information.
It analyzes and responds.
It is the mainframe station.

From the spinal cord and nerves
Command messages are sent out
To tell the organs and muscles,
"To take action without doubt."

# The Spinal Cord

Spinal cord is a bundle of nerves
Protected by the backbone.
Nearly forty-five miles of nerves
Travel from brain to each body zone.

They travel through the spinal cord.
It's about one-half inch wide,
Joins the brain at the base of the skull.
Spinal canal lodges it inside.

BZZZ
BZZZ

# *Symbols of America*

"Star-Spangled Banner,"
Our national anthem,
By Francis Scott Key,
For us to sing or hum.

Like the bald eagle,
Our land is free—
A symbol of freedom
For you and me.

Statue of Liberty,
Torch in her hand,
On Liberty Island
She does stand.

The Liberty Bell
On the fourth of July
Rang out for all—
The independence cry.

# Our Flag

Some call our
Flag "Old Glory."
Stars 'n stripes,
They tell a story.

Fifty stars for
Fifty states.
On a field of blue,
A star each rates.

Thirteen stripes for
The colonies first.
Hardy and true, they
Endured the worst.

# Pictures on Coins

Picture on a penny,
Abraham Lincoln.
One eye shows,
But he's not winkin'.

Picture on a nickel,
Thomas Jefferson.
Louisiana purchased
When he was done.

Picture on a dime,
Franklin Roosevelt.
Twelve years in office,
With depression dealt.

Picture on a quarter,
George Washington.
The first president,
Our Constitution won.

On the half-dollar
Is John F. Kennedy.
The presidential seal on
The other side we see.

# *Work Smarter,*
# *Not Harder*

Use your study time wisely.
Have a good frame of mind.
Work smarter, not harder—
A magic key, you'll find.

Plan your study time wisely.
Learn to estimate
The length of each assignment.
How much time does it rate?

Start your study time wisely,
With a brief review
Of what you have already learned.
It prepares you for the new.

Survey the chapter quickly.
Title, headings, and summary.
Look at all the pictures.
It's an overview, you see.

(Continued)

Have a purpose for your reading.
What do you need to know?
Read and think about each part.
In long-term memory it will go.

If the book belongs to you,
Important points you may highlight
In a color of your choice.
Make it outstanding and bright.

Test yourself as you review.
Important points you mind map.
Make up a memory crutch like
A song, jingle, rhyme, or rap.

Do your daily assignments.
Work carefully; be neat.
Make a time line; set goals.
Working smart cannot be beat!

# *Taking Notes*

Notes are for jogging your memory
Of speeches, films, thoughts, or reading.
Leave large margins to fill in later.
Note taking involves speeding.

Write so you can read it later.
Key words and phrases write.
Ask yourself, "Is this important?"
"Is there an author I should cite?"

Use colors, stars, and underline
Important points you need to know.
You can also use a mind map.
Note taking—way to go!

# *Mind Mapping*

Mind mapping is a system;
Pour ideas onto paper.
Enhances thinking skills—
It's a creative caper.

Mind mapping for your own use,
Mind mapping for your class—
Brains like to work this way.
Mind mapping is a gas!

Works for any subject;
Works for young and old.
Do it instead of outlines.
Try it out and you'll be sold.

Use a central image,
Key words, colors, codes.
No need to be an artist.
Use symbols and like modes.

When you start to mind map,
Create your own style,
Flexible and evolving.
Just try it for awhile.

# *Homework*

Set up a place to study.
Find a quiet spot,
A chair, a desk, or table.
A good light helps a lot.

Pencils, paper, pens
In a box or drawer,
So you can always find them
In your private store.

Choose a time for homework,
And keep it without fail.
You'll get into the habit.
Through the work you'll sail.

Congratulate yourself
When your homework's done.
Reward yourself for progress.
Relax and have some fun.

# *Study Skills*

Pay attention in class.
If you do not understand,
Ask questions. Don't be shy—
It's okay to raise your hand.

Write down all assignments
With their due dates near,
Which book, and what pages,
So that everything is clear.

Write down the assignments
On a special page or book.
Keep it in the same place;
You'll know just where to look.

Put assignment notes
And all the books you'll need
In a bag or backpack.
Organize, work smart, indeed.

When you arrive at home
At the end of the school day,
You'll have just what you need.
It's much easier that way.

# *Telephone Directory*

Telephone directory:
Names and addresses
And phone numbers.
No need for guesses.

Colored pages in
The telephone book
Give us clues
On where to look.

White pages
Phone numbers list,
Businesses and people.
Get the gist?

A product or a service
You need to know;
Use the yellow pages;
Find out where to go.

For the government
Try the blue pages,
To find an agency,
Taxes, rent, and wages.

Call the operator if
You need assistance.
Dial "O" to bill collect
When you call long distance.

# Emergency Telephone Number

A number to call
If help we need
Is 9 1 1.
They will pay heed.

Important number
Is 9 1 1—
For emergencies,
Not for fun!

For fire, police,
Or if someone is sick
And you need help;
They'll come quick.

If there is danger
To life or property,
Call 9 1 1;
They'll help, you see.

# *CLOSING*

I hope that you enjoy using this book as much as I have enjoyed writing it and seeing the method being used. I have always been passionately interested in watching children experience joyful learning.

We are living in an exciting time of change in education. As I travel around observing student teachers and presenting workshops for teachers and parents on Accelerated Learning, I am energized by their enthusiasm and desire to try new methods that brain research is finding to be more effective than some of the approaches used in the past.

I know from experience how busy and demanding days are for teachers (including home schoolers) and parents. If you have any suggestions regarding other areas of the curriculum for which you would like SmartRope jingles or SmartRaps, please contact me at the address below.

If you are using the material in this book successfully, please write. Nothing makes me happier than hearing of your successes. I am also interested in hearing your constructive criticism. What can I do to make Active Learning activities better or easier for you to use? I look forward to hearing from you. Write to:

Rosella Wallace
c/o Zephyr Press
P.O. Box 66006
Tucson, AZ 85728-6006

# BIBLIOGRAPHY

Anthony, Susan C. *Facts Plus: An Almanac of Essential Information.* Anchorage, Alaska: Instructional Resource Co., 1991.

Benne, Bart. *Waspleg and Other Mnemonics.* Dallas, Tex.: Taylor Publishing Co., 1988.

Benzwie, Teresa. *A Moving Experience.* Tucson, Ariz.: Zephyr Press, 1987.

Brewer, Chris, and Don G. Campbell. *Rhythms of Learning.* Tucson, Ariz.: Zephyr Press, 1991.

Caine, Nummela, and Geoffrey Caine. *Making Connections: Teaching and the Human Brain.* Association for Supervision and Curriculum Development, 1991.

Hart, Leslie. *Human Brain and Human Learning.* New York: Longman, 1983.

McCarthy, Bernice. *4MAT System: Teaching to Learning Styles with Right/Left Mode Techniques.* Barrington, Ill.: Excel Inc., 1987.

Margulies, Nancy. *Mapping Inner Space.* Tucson, Ariz.: Zephyr Press, 1991.

Miller, G. A. "The Magical Number Seven: Plus or Minus Two." *Psychological Review* 63 (1956): 81–97.

Ostrander, Sheila, and Lynn Schroeder. *Superlearning.* New York: Dell Publishing Co., 1979.

_____. *Supermemory: The Revolution.* New York: Carroll and Grof, 1991.

Peterson, Patricia. *The Know It All Resource Book for Kids.* Tucson, Ariz.: Zephyr Press, 1989.

Rose, Colin. *Accelerated Learning.* New York: Dell Publishing Co., 1985.

Wallace, Rosella. *Rappin' and Rhymin'.* Tucson, Ariz.: Zephyr Press, 1992.

_____. "Active Learning: A Practical Application of Current Learning Theories and Recent Relevant Brain Research to Elementary Education." Ph.D. Diss., Union Institute, 1989.

## Also by Rosella Wallace . . .

## RAPPIN' AND RHYMIN'

### Raps, Songs, Cheers, and SmartRope Jingles for Active Learning

**Rappin' and Rhymin'**

Raps, Songs, Cheers, and SmartRope™ Jingles for Active Learning

By Rosella R. Wallace, Ph.D.

by Rosella R. Wallace

Grades K–8

Optimize learning at home and in the classroom. Use the powers of rhythm and rhyme to teach children the information they need to know in a way they want to learn.

With *Rappin' and Rhymin'* you can—

- Motivate student participation
- Engage students in large-group response activities
- Provide enrichment, experience joy, and relieve stress

*80-page activity manual, 6" x 9", softbound; audiocassette with plastic case.*

**1028-W . . . $19.95**

## EDUCATION IN MOTION

### A Practical Guide to Whole-Brain Integration for Everyone

by Carla Hannaford, Cherokee Shaner, and Sandra Zachary

Grades K–12

Promote whole-brain and body integration with researched and tested exercises. You'll find the exercises effective and enjoyable for all learning styles and ages.

30-minute VHS video

**1703-W . . . $49**

---

## ORDER FORM    CALL, WRITE, OR FAX FOR YOUR FREE CATALOG!

| Qty. | Item # | Title | Unit Price | Total |
|------|--------|-------|-----------|-------|
| | 1028-W | Rappin' and Rhymin' | $19.95 | |
| | 1703-W | Education in Motion | $49 | |
| | | | | |

Name _____

Address _____

City _____

State _____ Zip _____

Phone (_____) _____

| | |
|---|---|
| Subtotal | |
| Sales Tax (AZ residents, 5%) | |
| S & H (10% of Subtotal, min. $3.00) | |
| Total (U.S. Funds only) | |

CANADA: add 22% for S& H and G.S.T.

**Method of payment (check one):**

❏ Check or Money Order    ❏ Visa

❏ MasterCard    ❏ Purchase Order attached

Credit Card No. _____

Expires _____

Signature _____

**Zephyr** Press ®

**To order write or call:**
P.O. Box 66006-W
Tucson, AZ 85728-6006
(602) 322-5090
FAX (602) 323-9402

**100% SATISFACTION GUARANTEE**
Upon receiving your order you'll have 90 days of risk-free evaluation. If you are not 100% satisfied, return your order within 90 days for a 100% refund of the purchase price. No questions asked!